T0128617

A BEGINNER'S GUIDE

HAIR WEAVE MANUAL

AVA BANTON

A BEGINNER'S GUIDE HAIR WEAVE MANUAL

iUniverse books may be ordered through booksellers or by contacting:

iUniverse
1663 Liberty Drive
Bloomington, IN 47403
www.iuniverse.com
844-349-9409

Because of the dynamic nature of the Internet, any web addresses or links contained in this book may have changed since publication and may no longer be valid. The views expressed in this work are solely those of the author and do not necessarily reflect the views of the publisher, and the publisher hereby disclaims any responsibility for them.

Any people depicted in stock imagery provided by Getty Images are models,
and such images are being used for illustrative purposes only.
Certain stock imagery © Getty Images.

ISBN: 978-1-6632-2857-4 (sc)
ISBN: 978-1-6632-2900-7 (e)

Library of Congress Control Number: 2021919760

Print information available on the last page.

iUniverse rev. date: 10/28/2021

CONTENTS

THE HAIR STYLIST: THANKFUL TESTIMONY

>—I—◆—O—◆—I—◁

In this beginner's weave manual, you will learn effective techniques for weave installations and hairstyles that were cultivated over years of experience in: sewing, gluing and weave placement. I hope you find the guide useful and have beautiful and natural results. Hair dressing is literally a tale about threads to me. The job is not all about hairstyles. It is about supporting the clients and appreciating the support they give. The job creates an environment with the kind of warmth equivalent to a community.

Over the years of working in the field I find the job to be both rewarding and supportive. When clients are satisfied and feel beautiful, I am rewarded by their smiles. I have developed relationships with great people who sit in my chair. They have shared messages about life that I have learned and grown from.

I love and appreciate my clients and enjoy forging connections through a vocation that is more than styling hair. It is about people who put their trust in my hands to create their vision.

God bless them all. Through them God blesses me. I thank God for them. May He continue to bless beyond the chair we share and I thank them for choosing me as their hairstylist.

Blessings to the hair stylist in you!

INSTALLATION TECHNIQUE

The installing of a weave is based on a combination of couple techniques, working together to get a unified result.

The foundation of the installation for desired hairstyle

o   The foundation determines the finish of the hairstyle and is therefore the most relevant factor to structure the weave,

The placement of install for desired hairstyle

o   Placing the hair requires more than stitching, tracking of gluing the hair, it also entails angling the weft of the weave. Placing install with a slightly upward curve, give shape to the angle in which the hair flows and helps define the individual facial features; giving easy accessibility to cut and style the weave in a finish that compliments the client's face.

The balancing of the recommended volume for desired hairstyle

o   Balancing is key, to the finish of installing the weave.

Using the recommended 3 bundles

- The crown takes the most of the portion of the weave and it is recommended one and quarter of the lot of bundles, while the other one and three quarters remainder of weave shared in two equal portions between the sides and back, which allows for a regular volume finish, and would need more bundles for a full volume, however, this process requires not only doubling up on the tracks, but recognizing where to place the double tracks

  i. And how to use stitch to lock weft in form hold, and accessible shape, ready to be cut into desired hairstyle, with the kind of security clients need to feel confident about their weaves.

DESIGN & STITCH PATTERNS

>–I◄►–O–◄►–I–◄

Types and Design Stitch and Patterns:

o   Stitch

Unless otherwise specified, sew from right to left if you are right-handed and from left to right if you are left-handed.

The Backstitch:

A very secure stitch used for weft that might be under more strain.

- Bring the needle up at side A
- Go behind your current stitch to side B
- Bring the needle out at area C just past you current stitch.

Knotting the thread:

- Take a small stitch, but do not pull thread all the way through.

- Stick your needle into the thread loop and pull until the loop is about an inch long.

- Stick the needle into the loop and wrap it around the thread twice.

- Pull the needle through.

- Do not cut the thread yet (you will want to hide the thread ends, if possible.)

If you are working with layered wefts you might be able to sandwich the thread where it will not be seen. To do this:

- Slide the needle between the layers and bring it out about an inch away.

- Pull the thread taut and cut it near the weft's surface. The cut thread should disappear into the weft. If you are not working with layers, just take a single stitch after you have knotted the thread, then cut it near the weft's surface.

The Shaping and Locking of the Stitch:

- Position the weft in the desired angle

- Bring your needle on top of the weft

- Pull all the way out from under, then bring needle under the stitch pulling through upward to the top

- Repeat by placing needle once again through the stitch from top

- Pull outward for the lock then cut thread.

WEAVE DESIGN

Variations of Weave Placement Design and the Recommended Distance between Tracks (1/2 inch):

Placement of weft half-inch apart allows for proper manageability and functionality of the weave and their effectiveness.

Sew-in placement

- Start by threading the needle and finish a heel knot on one end of the thread to achieve security between the thread and weft.
- With secured weft begin laying placement by stitching with the backstitch style throughout to a lock
- Glue-in Placement
- Carefully apply hair glue unto weft of weave
- Apply holding spray six inches away from the glue area.
- Using a blow dryer, semi-dry glue then begin placement and dry into a hold.
- Continue method throughout to secure a hold for a finish.

Provides instructions of methods for

- ➤ Securing a structured foundation for a modest finish
- ➤ Placement of installs effecting firm, shape and hold
- ➤ Balance volume with precise layers for desired finish

With distinct and detailed guidelines to successfully achieve smooth and natural looking bounce in beautiful sewn in or glue in weaves hairstyles.

My simple 3 **Steps** method will teach you to not only sew-in, but glue and track, weaves hair styles with natural exuberant finish and beautiful shines

A guide to weave perfection presents not one, not two but five basic pronounced hairstyles, plus a bonus; 'the art of mastering the Mohawk's shape and setting formation, in solid glowing maintainable finish.'

Hundreds of dollars of weave in instructions guaranteed to perfect hairstyles, all formatted in one single **3 steps** program

- • **The Back**
- • **The Sides**
- • **The Crown**

All simplified in quick and easy method with distinctive guidelines to get you installing sewn in, glue in or tracks, weave in record time.

Using five reputable styles, I have demonstrated simple effective technique for installing weaves that will keep its shape and form long after it is worn, and will sharpen weaving skill when followed correctly. I have not only provided diagrams with illustrated instructions but also detailed valuable information to take you through these quick and simple steps to perfect and effect firm, definitive beautiful weave installs as you get to craft and hone the skill crafting the skill. If you have the passion for weaves, with these steps can assist in your journey to becoming professional at weave installation. Even stylists may benefit from these fast and effective techniques and build upon them to establish their own techniques, creating, even a broader spectrum of the **3 steps** systems, all the time developing a skill worthy of a stable profitable income.

Using the **3 steps** method you will learn how to stitch or glue the hair to a firm hold, into whatever style desired, and get amazing natural effect of the finish that gives a beautiful shaped and styled flowing manage, all fall into desired design with the proportionate layer, volume and exuberance

Steps that get you precise volume, full bounce and flow the weave needs to shine for effect.

Steps that promise a smooth bump free, proportionately voluminous result.

Weaves that hold shape and is firm way past the six weeks' time limit recommendations

Follow the **steps** of combined experience and creative niche, combined, to formulate direct guides into easy and simple **steps** in perfecting a naturalized version of a complete styled and finesse, weaves.

With my quick and easy **steps** guide, you will not only learn how to formulate and install your tracks with lasting hold, low maintenance and free flows breath taking attention.

Also you will learn how to maximise your strategy in finding the right volume for the desired outcome and how to combine sewing ad shaping hair in place all at the same time, and it does not stop there, I will teach you the technique that locks stitch and hair into place, of desired hair design.

My **3 steps** plan gives you a step by step walk through a three section unit, all designed to simplify the installation of weave.

Step 1: The Base

The **base** defines the back of the style, which also is responsible for setting a foundation that creates a gateway for the fall of the flow of the hairstyles volume and finish.

Steps 2: The Sides

The **sides** define the angle of the style and are responsible for creating definitions for the way the style compliments the facial features, and sets up layers to effect appropriate volume, flow a finish.

Step 3: The Crown

The full head weave in all variations of styles centers upon the identification of the top center of the crown for approximation of finish, however the design.

The **crown** defines the front, and overall hairstyles finish and is responsible for effecting, precise, firm, smooth layering to compliment facial features for natural finesse finish, and is centered on identifying the top of the center, befitting the closure, which controls the shaping of the finished result, and can prove difficult to learn, when installing a full head weave if not properly aligned.

The full head though considered difficult and might be considered the most intricate of the three steps, when the top of the center is centered. The full head, to perfect is probably the most straight-forward to grasp.

Inside the '*Beginner's Guide: Hair Weave Manual*,' demonstrates how to break it all down into one single trace guide, a simple follow and finish circular path guide, where in you start install placement at bottom of the crown and finish at the top of the center, by way of building the volume of the style using the judgment of the shape of the angles provided by the base and the sides of the crown which allows for the install a format guide, a clear direct traceable accessibility wherein control of the weft placement makes for a simple steer of the circular frame almost instantaneously, creating possibilities for clear and precise lock to weave coverage.

Whether the crown is designed to affect a **close finished** hairstyle or naturalized precision in a **leave out** or the **side leave out**, a **middle leave out**, or the **horseshoe leave out**, the end result lies in aligning the layers with the individual shape of both the base and sides' foundation with this method. Using these steps you will be able to sew, glue or track on any style braids or caps. This technique teaches you to follow shape and size of the client's head to get the precise shape and volume for individual desired finish result.

Beautiful sewn track or glued in weaves installed to shape accessible formats for various styles, exuberating flows and manageable maintenance. With these quick and easy steps anyone can install a weave in record time. These techniques are effective in perfecting the art of installing weaves.

Crown-Full Head: Top Center Finish

This style requires the circular guide crown finish to perfect the install, and usually finish to bangs or sided sweep designs, such achievements is acquired by evaluating and formulating a circular guide, identifiable immediately on half inch on top of the sides' foundation to start the placement of the install using the one end of the weft to direct the placement into a circular guide, easily traced continue to align to the top center of the crown, a couple inches away from the designated lock, carefully steer the weft circling placement to a close and lock.

The Crown Leave Out

As opposed to installs for the close up crown, full head weave, with **leave out** designs, though the rows are easily traced and placed, with the back and sides foundations, hairstyles with leave outs, placement weft trace creates a gap, betwixt the start and finish below the top center of crown requiring layering to level the placement in a smooth line to effect designated finish. When sewing hairstyles with **leave out**, always bear in mind it is better to steer the placement aligned to the shape of the shape of the **leave out** section stitch the weft in a trace adjacent to the shape of the desired leave out hairstyle, doing this ensures the most effective trace guide flexible for placement of the layers and distribution for decisive hair coverage for the top crown **leave out** requires following the angle that the shape of the **leave out** itself created, as a direct guide for achieving effective results in framing *the* finish.

Crown-Side Part: Top Center Finish

Distribute weft's placement half inch immediately on top of side's foundation aligned with the shape of the **leave out** section and layer the gap section moderately for a decisive foundation for precise hair coverage finish.

Crown-Middle Part: Top Center Finish

Distribute weft's placement half inch immediately on top of side's foundation aligned with the shape of the **leave out** section and layer the gap section moderately for a decisive foundation for precise hair coverage finish.

Crown-Horseshoe Part: Top Center Finish

Distribute weft's placement half inch immediately on top of side's foundation aligned with the shape of the **leave out** section and layer the gap section for a decisive foundation for precise hair coverage finish.

Sides

Take the weft of the track. Place it in a slightly upward curve from the top taking the row into a straight line across the back ending with a slight curve to the top of side's end to achieve an angle for the weft which allows for a glowing flow of a hair fall on both sides of the weft with a lock stitch, continue with weft placement in a straight line inserting lock stitch throughout.

Back

- Take the weft of the hair and place the edge of the hair on the side of the back, preferably a doubled track, for setting up a full effective foundation, for the flow and volume of the hair's fall.
- Make a lock stitch continue placement with back stitch through to the other end insert a lock stitch
- Place another track using the above method for a second and third track

The Mohawk: Top Center Finish

Using top center, crown finish, and back guidelines, insert the zigzag stitch design on the sides; however, placing a double track at the back followed by single side track, immediately inserting the zigzag stitch design above the foundation, for the top center finish.`

One of the most effective ways of achieving the Mohawk sewing techniques is using the zigzag placement design, I had discovered from my many years of crafting the style, that this technique had proven to be very effective in setting the foundation for a quick and ready shaping of a Mohawk ready cut, and easily styled, finish.

Mostly used in Mohawk installation, the zigzag stitch, creates a fountain-fall formation shaping in a fringe end, with the perfect volume to blend into the desired thinning edge needed for precise finish on the sides for the distinctive Mohawk style weave, making the style easy and cut ready, for the Mohawk's finish.

While the zigzag technique prove perfect for weft's placement of the sides, it is also effective in setting a perfect downward fall for shaping the formation of a perfect angle to befit and define the facial features, and it is mostly effective in creating a perfect fringe end, that sets up the thinning for immediate smooth sides needed to set a balance volume with accessibility cut and style to ready, to be styled to perfect finish, ready to be topped off, with a mini top center crown full head double tracked, singled down at the very end for the lock; and the front placement, in an exuberant effect.

With this technique the sides definitively and distinctly reveals a quick and ready to be easily styled into a Mohawk.

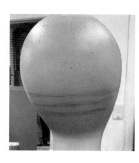

Back

Double

Single track

Single track

Crown with middle part

Double

Single

Layer

Leave out shape finish

Sides

Double track

Single

Single

Crown full head

Back method

Sides- method

Crown top center finish

Crown with side part

Double

Single

Layer

Leave out shape finish

Crown with horseshoe part

Double

Single

Layer

Leave out shape finish

Front

Double across

Single

Single

Crown top center finish

Mohawk

Back

Double track

Mohawk

Sides

Single track

Zigzag stitch design

ILLUSTRATIONS

BACK

CENTER LEAVE OUT

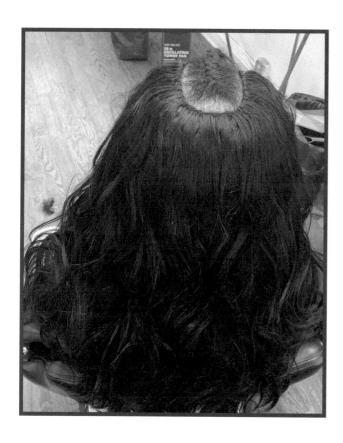 

SIDE LEAVE OUT

 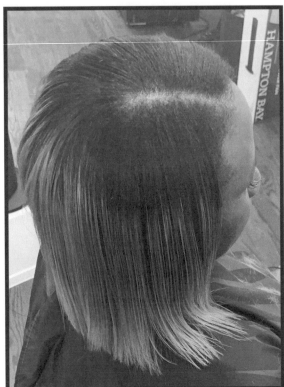

HORSESHOE

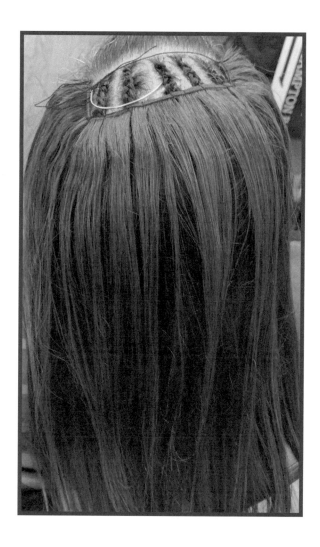

FULL HEAD

 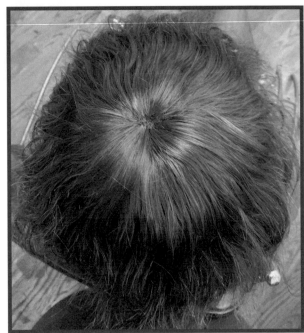

MOHAWK

BANG FINISH

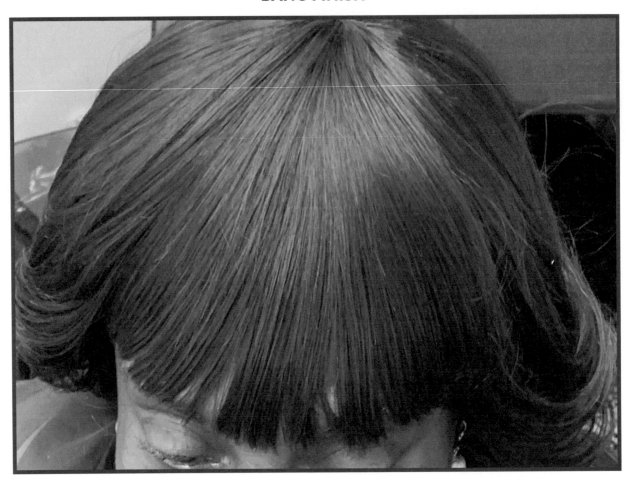

SIDE FINISH